THE little

TO

50

Aubrey Malone

www.booksbyboxer.com

Published in the UK by
Books By Boxer, Leeds, LS13 4BS
© Books By Boxer 2015
All Rights Reserved

ISBN: 9781909732018

Yahoo!

At last you're

50

DON'T WORRY!!!

Here's some expert advice to help you get through it!

The secret of staying young is to live honestly, eat slowly and lie about your age.

(Lucille Ball)

My husband gave me
an elaborate dinner set
for my last birthday...
50 toothpicks!

My age is 39 plus tax.

(Liberace)

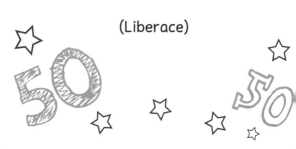

50 ☆ ☆ ☆ 50 ☆

☆

You're getting old
when the only thing
you don't want for
your birthday is to be
reminded of it.

☆

☆

☆

Whenever the subject
of age comes up,
she gets shy...
about ten years shy!

The years that a woman
subtracts from her age
aren't lost, they're added
on to other women's.

(Diane de Poitiers)

You know you're old
when everybody goes
to your birthday party
and stands around the
cake just to get warm.

(George Burns)

She reaches her age
by light years – she's
sure light a few years.

(Henny Youngman)

I'm pleading with my wife to have birthdays again. I don't want to grow old alone.

(Rodney Dangerfield)

I´ve found the
secret of youth...
I lie about my age.

(Joey Adams)

50

A youthful figure is
what you get when you
ask a woman her age.

She's the demure type. Demure she gets older, demure she conceals it.

50 50 50 50

Ladies...
don't worry about
losing your youth.
Strap him to the
bedpost instead.

From birth to 18 a girl needs parents. From 18 to 35 she needs good looks. From 35 to 55 she needs a good personality. From 55 on she needs good cash.

(Sophie Tucker)

With a little practice
any woman can
remain thirty years
old at every birthday.

I believe in loyalty. I think when a woman reaches an age she likes she should stick to it.

(Eva Gabor)

50

I've just hit fifty.
That means it takes
me all night to do
once what I once
used to do all night.

Yes, I'd consider
going out with
women my age...
if there WERE any!

(George Burns at 92)

If you survive long
enough you're
revered – rather like
an old building.

(Katharine Hepburn)

Advanced old age
is when you sit in
a rocking chair and
can't get it going.

(Eliakim Katz)

Old age is the happiest
time in a man's life.
The trouble is, there's
so little of it.

(W.S. Gilbert)

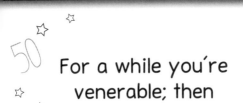

For a while you're
venerable; then
you're just old.

(Lance Alworth)

It's not how old you are, it's how hard you work at it.

(Jonah Barrington)

Old age is always
15 years older than
what I am.

(Bernard Baruch)

50

The trouble is you're not allowed to grow old in the world anymore.

(Tony Hancock)

Old age isn't so bad
when you consider
the alternative.

(Maurice Chevalier)

Old age takes away
what we've inherited
and gives us what
we've earned.

(Gerald Brennan)

Youth is a disease from
which we all recover.

(Dorothy Fuldheim)

A senior moment is a
euphemism people use
to indicate temporary
loss of marbles to
anyone over 50.

(Spike Milligan)

You can calculate Zsa Zsa Gabor's age by the rings on her fingers.

(Bob Hope)

If you live to be 100,
you've got it made.
Very few people die
past that age.

(George Burns)

Growing old is like being increasingly penalised for a crime you haven't committed.

(Anthony Powell)

Birthdays only come
once a year, unless
you're Joan Collins.
In which case they
only come once
every FOUR years.

One of the good things
about getting older is
that you find you're more
interesting than most of
the people you meet.

(Lee Marvin)

Bob Hope is so old,
when he first started
going to school, history
wasn't even a subject.

Old age and
treachery
beats youth
and vitality.

The four stages of
man are infancy,
childhood, adolescence
and absolescence.

(Art Linkletter)

There are three signs
of old age - you
forget names, you
forget faces and...

(Red Skelton)

We were planning to count the candles on his birthday cake, but we were driven back by the heat.

(Stuart Turner)

When I turned 50 I had
my prostate checked.
What a pain in the arse.

(Bob Geldof)

I was brought up to respect my elders, but I can't find any of them anymore.

(George Burns on his 90th birthday)

No matter how old a mother is, she watches her middle-aged sons for signs of improvement.

(Helen Rowland)

Zsa Zsa Gabor has discovered the secret of eternal middle age.

(Oscar Levant)

50 is the age at which food becomes more important than sex.

(Pru Leith)

He's so old, his birth certificate is carved on a ROCK.

(Jack Benny)

50 ☆ ☆ ☆ **50**

☆ ☆

Except for an
occasional heart
attack, I feel as
☆ young as I ever did.

(Robert Benchley)

When I was young I was told, "You'll see when you're 50." Well, now I'm 50 and I haven't seen a thing.

(Erik Satie)

Getting on in years
means suffering the
morning after when
you haven't even had
the night before.

(Henny Youngman)

I haven´t asked you
to make me younger.
All I want is to go on
getting older.

(Konrad Adenauer
to his doctor)

As a graduate of the
Zsa Zsa Gabor School of
Creative Mathematics,
I honestly do not know
how old I am.

(Erma Bombeck)

If you live long enough
you get accused of
things you never did
and praised for virtues
you never had!

(I.F. Stone)

All would live long,
but none would be old.

(Benjamin Franklin)

50

An old man gives good
advice to console himself
for no longer being able
to set a bad example.

(Duc de la Rochefoucauld)

The tragedy of old age
is not that one is old,
but that one is young.

(Mark Twain)

My ambition in life
is to stop being an
adolescent after 50.

(Wendy Cope)

Old guys of 50 plus
love me with a whip
in my hand.

(Anne Robinson)

Anyone can get old.
All you have to do is
live long enough.

(Groucho Marx)

If I'd known I was
going to live this long,
I'd have taken better
care of myself.

(Adolph Zukor)

50

There are certain signs that you're getting on in years. I walked past the cemetery the other day and two guys ran after me with shovels.

(Rodney Dangerfield)

He's so old, his
blood type has
been discontinued.

(Bill Dana)

The man who views the world at 50 the same as he did at 30 has wasted 20 years of his life.

(Muhammad Ali)

It is obscene to think
that one day one will look
like an old map of France.

(Brigitte Bardot)

First you forget names,
then you forget faces.
Then you forget to
zip your fly. Then you
forget to unzip your fly.

(American baseball
manager Branch Rickey
on the perils of ageing)

Nowadays, when a fan runs up to me, it's not to get my autograph but to have a better look at my wrinkles.

(Liz Taylor)

Growing old is
something you do
if you're lucky.

(Groucho Marx)

When you're green
you're growing, when
you're ripe, you're not.

(Ray Kroc)

In youth we run into
difficulties. In old age,
difficulties run into us.

(Josh Billings)

You know you're
getting old when the
candles cost more
than the cake.

(Bob Hope)

50 50 50 50 50

Every morning
when I get up, I
read the obituary
page. If my name
isn't in it, I shave.

(George Burns)

I'm 65 and I guess that puts me in with the geriatrics. But if there were 15 months in every year, I'd only be 48. That's the trouble with us. We number everything. Take women for example. I think they deserve to have more than 12 years between the ages of 28 and 40.

(James Thurber)

The three ages of man
are young, old and "You're
looking wonderful!"

(Jack Lynch)

You're only as old as the
woman you're feeling.

(Groucho Marx)

50

I'm so old I knew
Madame Butterfly when
she was a caterpillar.

(Bob Hope)

50 50

Sex at 50 is certainly better than at 51. That's the house next door.

(Bob Monkhouse)

When you're old,
everything you do is
sort of a miracle.

(Millicent Fenwick)

When we speak about
people of a certain age,
what we mean is people
of an UN-certain age.

I've got to the age where I need my false teeth and my hearing aid before I can ask where I've left my glasses.

(Stuart Turner)

If you want to make a
success of old age, you
have to start young.

(Fred Astaire)

I'd hate to tell you how old I am, but I reached the age of consent 75,000 consents ago.

(Shelley Winters)

He's so old that when he orders a 3 minute egg, they ask for the money up front.

(Milton Berle)

The only thing that bothers me about growing older is that when I see a pretty girl now it arouses my memory instead of my hopes.

(Milton Berle)

The secret of longevity
is to keep breathing.

(Sophie Tucker)

At 50, confine your piercings to sardine cans.

(Joan Rivers)

She's a woman of a
certain age -
the Stone Age.

There are so many ways of dying. It's astonishing that any of us choose old age.

(Beryl Bainbridge)

The hardest years
in life are between
10 and 70.

(Helen Hayes)

50 is the age at which a man discovers he only needs one suit.

(Clifton Fadiman)

50

50

By the time you reach my age you've made plenty of mistakes if you've lived your life properly.

(Ronald Reagan)

I've been 40 and I've been 50 and I can tell you 40 is better.

(Cher)

The older I get, the
better I used to be.

(John McEnroe)

Actresses who say being over 50 is great are lying. I may look good, but I looked better at 32. No, it's not great being over 50. It's like going to the guillotine.

(Angie Dickinson)

40 is the first time
you realise you can't
do it the second time.
50 is the second time
you realise you can't
do it the first time.

(Mort Sahl)

Remember...
It could be worse!
You could be 60!